Are You Scaring Him Away?

How to keep a guy,

by not doing,

what you do

By

Kathy Shantel

Are You Scaring Him Away? How to keep a guy, by not doing, what you do

Copyright © 2017

All rights reserved. This book or any portion thereof may not be reproduced or used in any manner whatsoever without the express written permission of the publisher except for the use of brief quotations in a book review.

ISBN: 9781520239996

Warning and Disclaimer

Every effort has been made to make this book as accurate as possible. However, no warranty or fitness is implied. The information provided is on an "as-is" basis. The author and the publisher shall have no liability or responsibility to any person or entity with respect to any loss or damages that arise from the information in this book.

Publisher contact

Skinny Bottle Publishing

books@skinnybottle.com

Introduction

Have you ever gone out with a guy, only to have him dump you a few dates later? Do you find it hard to get a boyfriend? Has your boyfriend left you for no apparent reason? And how about that friend of yours who seems to be luckier than you—what is she doing differently?

Don't feel bad. It happens to many women. If you are doing things that scare guys away, it is because no-one ever told you what these things are. But you are about to find out.

This book will put everything you need to know in your head so that, if you ever scare a guy away again, you are only doing it on purpose.

Knowing this stuff is easy, and putting it in practice is no big deal either. You just have to identify what you are doing wrong and stop doing it. You don't have to transform yourself in the process. This book is about getting what you want, not giving men what they want.

After all, women and men are two different animals. For a woman and a man to get along, something's got to give on both sides. Men want to be loved just as women do, and that means they will put up with some of your stuff.

And the surprising good news is that if you acknowledge your misbehavior, you will immediately stick out from the crowd—you will become special.

But how do you know in advance what constitutes misbehavior in a guy's head? It's easy. To identify what you are doing wrong, you just read through the book and check when you find a behavior that you recognize as yours. Make a list on a piece of paper. If something doesn't seem like a big deal, or you don't think it bothers your guy, keep a note of that too. It could be the deal breaker you have been missing all along.

From now and on, you will know exactly what not to do if you want to turn your date into a boyfriend, or your boyfriend into a loving husband.

What scares a guy away

If you are in a relationship and you feel your guy drifting away, or if you are seeing a guy and he seems to be avoiding you after a few dates, then you should start asking yourself why that is before it's too late.

Saying "I love you" too soon or too often—and expecting him to do the same

Who does not like hearing the words "I love you?" Everyone longs to be loved, but these words should be spoken to the right person and at the right time. Say it too soon to a guy and he'll probably run towards the other direction. Say it too often to your guy and he could get tired of hearing it.

Too soon and you'll drive him away

Dating a man does not automatically mean that he loves you. As a woman, you are vulnerable and you may not able to control your feelings as well as men do. But blurting out "I love you" after a couple of dates would scare a guy away. Wouldn't it feel better if he says it first?

After all, isn't that the way it should be? Having the guts to approach a man and ask him out for a drink is not the same as telling him that you love him. There is a limit to being bold. Let him make the next move. Give him the chance to be a man.

Let the relationship grow and develop before you start expressing your feelings to him. If he cares for you, he will show it and spell out the words himself.

So, try to chill out and enjoy spending time with him. Enjoy his company. Enjoy his attention. Do not push him away by telling him that you love him when you know that he isn't ready for it yet. How do you know he is ready? He is ready when he tells you himself.

Too often and you will drive him nuts

Everyone knows how important it is to express your love with your partner. Simply saying "I love you" is one of the best ways of letting him know how you feel about him. And of course, you would expect him to say those words back to you.

In the beginning of a relationship, uttering those words can be the sweetest thing for both of you. But after a while—though you still want to keep on saying them—your guy could start growing tired of hearing or saying "I love you".

Yes, it can be annoying. But, you have to understand that for some men, these words are no longer important when they believe they've already shown their women how much they care.

And if you try to push it by asking him if he loves you, you would probably end up with an answer that goes like this: "Why ask when you already know the answer." Or worse, he could answer with a yes but without the emotion that should go with it.

If that happens, you would be more annoyed and you could start getting sarcastic. What do you think his reaction would be? He would either laugh at you and not take you seriously, or he would start getting annoyed himself.

You have to understand that men are different from women when it comes to expressing their love. It is understandable that you want to keep the fire burning by making him aware of your feelings and making sure that he still loves you. Sometimes though, you should also consider the things he does for you and not just the words that he says.

Men are unpredictable. What they do may surprise you. Wouldn't it be better to just let him say those words when he really feels like doing so? That way, when he does, you would know for sure that he means it.

On your part, maybe you should try to stop saying "I love you" too often. Though it's sweet, your guy could be a little tired of hearing it. Also, he may feel pressured every time you do.

Make him miss you saying those words. He already knows that you love him. And though he was excited to hear you say it the first few times, be assured that he wouldn't want to hear it a dozen times a day. He knows. And you should know too. Don't expect him to say it every time you want reassurance of his love.

Be content. Be happy. Be confident of his love. Words would be meaningless if repeatedly uttered.

Getting paranoid over stupid little things

This attitude could scare away a guy you are with or someone you are just dating. Paranoia is bad. There are times though when it cannot be avoided. If you keep suspecting that something is not right, then you will end up getting anxious over little things. Relax and calm down. There is light at the end of the tunnel.

Irrational jealousy

Jealousy is not healthy. No matter how many times you've told yourself that being jealous is proof of being in love; it is never going to help you with your relationship.

Sometimes, being jealous is normal. But what if you are getting jealous more often than you should? Do you know when your jealousy has crossed the line? Or has jealousy blinded you, and you cannot think rationally.

Men like women who are confident, and being irrationally jealous is a clear sign of insecurity. If you are always freaking out when he's not doing what he's supposed to be doing, then you are doing a good job scaring him away. You are effectively fighting his attraction towards you.

Women should understand that men are sensitive too. Though they tend to present cool and nonchalant images, they do pick up quickly on psycho girlfriends. So, you better send away your inner demons and cast away your jealous nature before the damage cannot be undone.

Missed calls and late responses

If you are hanging out with a guy and you start making a fuss over silly little things, chances are he will think of you as paranoid and not a good potential girlfriend. There are of course legit situations for you to get mad.

But if he just missed a call or did not respond to a text message, you should try to control your anger and give him some slack. After all, he could be busy doing something important. Don't you get busy sometimes? Don't you make late responses too? Do not expect him to be glued on his phone all the time, even if you are.

Canceled plans and forgotten anniversaries

If your guy cancels a plan, it is alright to be annoyed for a while. But before you start nagging, try to know why the plan was canceled. He could have a valid reason for his decision. If that is the case, do not get mad and show understanding.

Men, for some reason, cannot seem to remember anniversaries. As a woman, you have to realize that you will have to remind him about such things. If your anniversary is approaching and your guy is not showing signs of remembering it, just give him some hints. Do not just sulk and start a fight. If you do, you may not have any more anniversaries.

Hanging out with the guys

This is the most common thing that usually drives women nuts. Men will always want to hang out with their buddies. Women want to hang out with their girlfriends too, but their desire might not be as strong. Try not to nag him every time he tells you that he will hang out with the boys.

Be happy that he lets you know where he is going. If he stops giving you updates about his activities, then that could be a sign that something is wrong. He could be doing something behind your back, or he simply does not want you nagging him every time he wants to go out with his friends.

Checking his social media accounts or email

Stalking a guy on social media is a big no-no if you want him to stick around. If you consistently ask about the women who "like" or comment on his posts, he might end up deleting you. Argue with him about it and he might even block you.

It does not matter if he is your boyfriend already or if you want him to be—you have to give him some privacy. If you are in his circle and you can view his profile, then he most likely wants you to see what you are seeing.

Do not give him a reason to avoid you on social media. How would you feel if you suddenly stopped seeing his updates? Has he stopped updating his profile or has he filtered you out? When he eventually does the latter, it could only mean that you are starting to scare him off.

Being clingy and possessive

It is only natural that you would want to spend as much time as possible with your guy. However, this does not mean that you two have to stay together all the time. Even if he is your husband or you live together, there will be times when you and he will need some space.

The same thing applies to a potential boyfriend—maybe even more so. Dating someone does not imply keeping him tied to your waistline. No man wants to be owned, so make him feel like he's free. The more you cling, the more he will try to pull away.

Allow him to have the freedom to do the things he loves. If he starts feeling restrained by you, it won't be long before he loses interest and leaves. Relationships flourish when both partners can keep doing what they were doing before, for the most part.

Asking to hang out all the time

When a man asks you out, it means that he likes you. But, that does not make him exclusively yours. You have to understand that if you agree to go out with him, you are just agreeing that you want to get to know him better. So, do not push him away by demanding more time. Wanting to hang out with him at every possible moment will make him skeptical.

Men like women who have other interests and social activities. If you are constantly asking him to spend time with you, you are showing him just how boring your life is without him.

One of the most common things women do when they are dating seriously is to stay away from friends and focus on their relationships. That's the wrong move. What's going to happen if things do not work out with you and the guy you are dating? If you ignore your buddies because you are in love, do you think they will be there for you if you get dumped? If a man senses that you are so much dependent on him, he is likely to be turned off.

If a man wants to hang out with you, he will ask you. Though men like to be chased sometimes, they still like to think that they are in control. That is why, it is better to let them do the asking most of the time. As a woman, the best thing you can do is to lead him into asking you to hang out. Try not to suffocate him with endless invitations to go here and there. Do not give him the excuse to avoid you, because he might do that even though he does not want to, if you start acting like a possessive wife.

Being too inquisitive

Can't help asking too many questions? If you have to be inquisitive, try to be cool about it, even if what you really want to do is to scream out the questions in his face. Too many questions at one occasion will quickly drive a guy away.

There are polite questions and there are annoying questions. If you are curious about something, think of the question first. You can ask him something like: "How was your last night?" even though what you really want to ask is: "Who were you with last night?" The first question may not give you the specific answer that you want, but the way he reacts may be more revealing than what he actually says.

Follow up questions are for interviews alone. So, try not to use them unless necessary. Asking questions like: "Were you with another girl?" and "What time did you finally come home?" would only make you sound insecure and possessive. Stop yourself before he starts running to avoid your next question.

Showing up "accidentally" at places where he hangs out

This can be annoying. If he lets you know where his going, it means that he trusts you. It does not mean that you should stalk him while he's having a good time with his friends. If he wanted you there, he would invite you.

Arriving uninvited is not going to make you look good on his book. Imagine what his friends would think of you or him. Do not "accidentally" show up, wait to be invited.

Claiming him on social media

Unless with agreement, try not to claim him on social media. Doing so would pressure him to do the same and if he's not up to that, he might break up with you. Men do often deactivate their social media when they start feeling annoyed with their women.

If you are just dating the guy, control yourself from acting as if he is yours on social media. If you want to post pictures of you together, just ask him, but do not make a big deal out of it. If you want to freak him out, the best way is by adding his friends and commenting on all of his posts.

Calling or texting too often

One text message is enough. Wait for his reply. If you have something important to tell him, call him once. If he did not take the call or if he's busy, leave him a message. Try to calm down and relax. Eventually, he will return the call or text back.

Calling and texting too often will not get his attention. Instead, it will make him feel stalked and harassed. Men have the tendency to get easily annoyed when women demand constant communication. They also tend to pull away when women demand more of their time.

Never go overboard with your messages and calls. If you do not know where to draw the line, it is better to send one too few messages than one too many. Make him miss your messages and your calls.

Pushing your friends on him

One of the most common mistakes a woman makes is assuming the guy she's dating is interested in meeting her friends. Avoid pushing your friends on him too soon. Even after a couple of dates, the guy is still trying to get to know you. Introducing a guy you are dating to your friends is like putting him on display as the "boyfriend." That's putting too much pressure on him.

Pushing your friends on him may make him think that you are pressuring him to commit. And if he's not yet ready for that, introducing him to your friends could be the last thing you would do with him.

Let him enjoy the time with you and if things between the two of you work out fine, he will be more than willing to get to know your friends.

Being too inconsistent—to the point of lying

It is hard to keep an affair if one or both of you are inconsistent with your statements. Most men would appreciate the truth even if it is not good.

Some women think that they have to play games with every guy they meet. That is not true. Inconsistency and lying can poison a relationship faster than anything else.

Do not be all over him for a week and then suddenly decide that you want to keep your distance the following week. He will be totally confused and probably wonder if you are seeing someone else.

On the other hand, you do not have to be totally consistent. If you always act the way he expects you to, things can get boring. Small surprises help keep a relationship alive. Just don't overdo it, and don't let him hanging for too long.

Giving misleading information

Don't tell a guy you like doing something and then retract that statement later. Though you may think it's cute, it can hurt your image substantially. If you always tell the truth, you will not have to remember what you told him in the past.

It is understandable that you might want to enhance your image, especially if you are very interested in somebody. If you are hoping for a long-term relationship with that guy, he will eventually find out if you gave him misleading information. What do you think he would do in that case?

Keeping secrets

It is alright not to disclose all your personal details to someone that you are just dating. And it is alright to have secrets. After all, both of you are at a stage where mystery is still exciting.

However, being mysterious is different from not telling the truth when you ought to. You can keep the mystery in some aspects, but when he wants to know about something important that he should know about, you better tell him. If you don't and he finds out the truth from another source, he is likely to leave you.

Trash-talking anyone

Women like gossip, and though some men are into it as well, they do have their own set of rules when it comes to talking about other people. When men gather around to discuss other people's lives, they talk about it sensibly. No judgment, no trash-talking, just simple discussion about stories they hear.

With women though, every story is a juicy gossip. If you want to discuss other people, talk to your girlfriends. Leave your boyfriend, or the guy you are dating, out of it. He'd rather not be bothered with all the drama.

When you are out with a guy, do not to talk about your friends' lives, your ex's failings, your roommate's bed partners, etc. If you spend the entire date trash talking, he might never ask you out again.

Some men simply dump women for creating too much drama. Don't think you are an exception. Push him too far with your gossips and he may not think twice about telling you that he does not want to see you again. Actually, you would be lucky if he is generous enough to let you know.

Bad-mouthing the exes

Talking about your exes is not a good thing to do with your new date or boyfriend. A little discussion about your ex or his ex should be okay if you both agree to talk about it. But, after a few exchanges of the good and the not-so-good experiences, you both should move forward and concentrate on each other.

Whatever you do, do not talk crap about an ex-boyfriend. That man was someone you were in love with at some point in your life. You invited him into your life. You shared your time with him. So, even if you are right, bad-mouthing him will only make your new date think less of you.

Discussing your friends' secrets

You know your friends' secrets because they trusted you with such confidential and sensitive matters. Discussing them with your guy would probably make him think that you are not a trustworthy person. Don't plant a seed of doubt in his mind about your trustworthiness. Guys usually treat this stuff more seriously than women.

If he asks about a friend, just give him the most basic information. Avoid divulging too much. After all, you have no right to discuss your friends' private lives, even with your boyfriend.

Complaining about his friends

If he introduced you to his friends and you do not find them nice or you think they do not approve of you, the best thing that you can do is to keep your mouth shut. They are his friends and not yours.

The fact that you have been introduced to them means that he thinks you are special. One bad word about his friends and he might start having second thoughts. Give it time. Your first impression of his friends may eventually change, and vice versa.

Remember to stop yourself from complaining about his friends or the way they treated you. Otherwise, you may end up on his "friends" list yourself.

Talking about the "future"

If you are dating a guy for a while and you things are going well, then you are one of the lucky ones. Do not spoil what you have by suddenly talking about having a "future" with him. Let him be the one to open that subject.

Though it is nice to have a clear idea where the relationship is going, it may be unwise to put pressure on him to commit. It would be better to let the relationship evolve and develop naturally.

If he cares for you and values you, he will commit when he's ready, not when he is pressured to do it. If you think he's not likely to commit any time during this lifetime, you have the option to be the one to walk away. Just accept the facts and don't force the issue.

Even if this is only about being "future-oriented" rather than committing, guys have a knee-jerk reaction when women bring up these subjects. Play it safe and let him worry about the future, if you want to have a future at all.

Fishing for compliments

If the guy said you're pretty, just smile and be happy. Do not ask him if he thinks you are pretty a few minutes after he said you were. That's fishing and men simply hate that, especially if they have already acknowledged and announced the obvious.

It is important to remember that when a man you are dating says: "You look beautiful." he really means it. He would not be dating you if he does not see how pretty you are. So, be content with one compliment.

Do not fish for compliments. Let his compliments come from his heart. If you keep on asking him about how he sees you or how he feels about you, you will only manage to frustrate him and achieve the opposite of what you were hoping for.

How to tell if you scared him off

Is he starting to drift away? Are you finding it hard to keep track of him? Is he getting out of your radar? A scared man is not going to stay around. This chapter is about how to find out if you have successfully freaked him out.

Not saying "I love you" at all

If this is a date, this does not apply.

If he was into expressing his love for you at the start, you have to remember that he was doing that to convince you. Once you are in a relationship with him, he will probably stop being too vocal about his feelings. That shouldn't alarm you though, as men are usually like that.

You should be concerned though if he totally stops saying "I love you". This could mean that he is no longer in love and that you have scared him off.

Avoiding your calls and not responding to your messages

You call and he does not pick up. You message and he does not respond. Face it girl, he's one scared bloke.

Hopefully, you did not completely scare him off. So give him some time to gather his thoughts. He might eventually realize that he still cares for you and decide to give the relationship another shot.

Hanging out with his friends more often

If your boyfriend suddenly has more time for his friends than for you, he might want to distance himself from you, even if for a little while. Men who are happy with their relationships make an effort to spend most of their time with their women.

If he's not doing that anymore, you either have to give him the space he needs or prepare yourself for the incoming breakup.

Coming up with many excuses not to be with you

Men can always come up with excuses. If a guy does not want to be with a girl, no amount of persuasion can make him change his mind. But you can be assured that he can come up with a different excuse for every occasion.

If he starts saying that he's too busy with work when he was not a week ago—that could be an excuse. If he is suddenly always unavailable in the weekends, do not expect him to stick around for long.

Deactivating social media account

This could be the ultimate sign of a very scared guy. If your date blocks you from his social media (rather than simply unfriend you), you might have done something very scary indeed.

If you can no longer see him on your social media, expect him to disappear from your life too. The signals are clear. He is scared and he is not to be found.

Conclusion

There is no such thing as a perfect relationship. You may have been going through some rough times with your boyfriend and you are not sure about what caused the bumpy ride. The best thing you can do is to evaluate the relationship, his current attitude towards you and the way you treat him.

Ladies, dating is a game—an awkward game. Everyone has been there: you get your flirt on and you think you've got something good going. And then, out of nowhere, a switch gets flipped and either you have been friend-zoned or the guy simply disappeared. That seriously sucks. You are left feeling confused, and sad.

Usually, women have no idea for the sudden changes in their dating partners' attitude. You may be so absorbed in analyzing your partner that you've missed the main point. You could be doing something silly that he could not come to terms with. Face it—if this has been happening to you since your teenage years something is wrong.

You may not be aware that your guy feels annoyed with you because you are too focused on trying to keep the fire burning. But, how are you doing that? By making sure that he's always by your side? By knowing all his moves and decisions? By keeping tabs on his friends? By asking too many questions? By texting and calling too often? By telling him that you love him with every chance you get? By being too jealous of everything?

None of this is going to make him stay. To keep him you have to give him the chance to get to know you without being too pressured into doing anything other than what he wants. Just let everything run. Do not force the relationship to go anywhere. If it is supposed to work, it will.

But it should take the two of you working together to make it work. Do not put too much effort unless he is showing signs of getting serious.

One of the main reasons women start to feel jealous, insecure and paranoid about men is because they have assumed too much from the start. If you stay cool about everything, you will prevent yourself from doing things that could scare your guy away. So, chill out. Relax. Enjoy having him around for however long you do, and it might just be forever.

Win a free

kindle
OASIS

Let us know what you thought of this book to enter the sweepstake at:

http://booksfor.review/scaringhim

Printed in Great Britain
by Amazon